Just a Game

Written by Adam and Charlotte Guillain

It was Saturday afternoon. Finn and Tess went to call for their friends.

"Let's play football!" shouted Finn as they ran onto the grass.

Finn quickly scored a goal.

"We can win this!" he called to Stefan and Asha.

Finn passed to Stefan but he picked up
the football.

"I saw this brilliant video!" said Stefan. "Someone was doing this!" He put the ball on his finger and started to spin it.

"Wow!" said Tess. "Can I try?"

Tess had a go, then Sophie tried, and then Asha.

"Hey!" cried Finn. "We're playing a match!"

They started playing again. Tess kicked
the football but Asha cut across Sophie and
passed to Stefan. He flicked the ball up with
his heels.

"That's brilliant!" called Rav.

"Thanks!" said Stefan. "I saw this trick on a video, too."

"Can I try?" said Rav.

Stefan flicked the ball to Rav.

They began taking it in turns to try the trick.
When Tess took the ball, Finn shouted,
"Stop that! We're playing a match!"

"It's just a game," muttered Tess as she kicked the ball to Rav. Rav sprinted towards the goal and scored.

"One all," said Finn.

The next time Stefan got the ball, he started
to bounce it like a basketball player.

"Hey, that's against the rules!" cried Finn.

Stefan threw the ball to Asha.

"Stop!" shouted Finn. "You're not playing properly!"

"It's just a game!" said Stefan.

It's not the World Cup!

Finn grabbed the ball and ran with it towards the goal. He scored and cheered, "Two–one to my team!"

"That's not fair!" cried Sophie.

"I thought it was *just a game*," replied Finn.
He stormed indoors with the football.

"Oh dear," said Asha. "What should we do?"

While the others played, Stefan kept looking at the flats.

"I feel bad for annoying Finn," he told Asha.

"Maybe you should go and find him?" said Asha.
Stefan nodded and ran inside.

The girls were teaching Rav to do cartwheels on the lawn when they heard shouting.

"Is that Finn and Stefan?" asked Sophie.

They ran inside the flat.

"Please don't argue!" Tess called as she pushed open Finn's bedroom door.

"We're not arguing," said Finn. He had
the football spinning on his finger.
"Go on, Finn!" shouted Stefan.

That's why we could
hear shouting!

"It's a new record," said Stefan, pressing his stopwatch. "You're better than me!"

"It doesn't matter who's better," said Finn. "It's just a game!"

Talk about the story

Answer the questions:

1 On what day did the story happen?

2 What did Stefan do with the ball first?

3 Why did Finn storm indoors?

4 Why did the friends run inside to find Finn and Stefan?

5 Why is it important for games to have rules?

6 Have you ever had to say sorry to a friend? What happened?

Can you retell the story in your own words?